The Blessing
Ramadan

Javed Ali

GOODWORD
goodwordbooks.com

يَٰٓأَيُّهَا ٱلَّذِينَ ءَامَنُوا۟ كُتِبَ

عَلَيْكُمُ ٱلصِّيَامُ كَمَا كُتِبَ عَلَى ٱلَّذِينَ مِن قَبْلِكُمْ

لَعَلَّكُمْ تَتَّقُونَ

"O You who have attained to faith!
Fasting is ordained for you
as it was ordained for those before you,
so that you might remain conscious of God."
The Qur'an (2:183)

Photographic credits:
Peter Sanders, 30, 40; Kabir Khan, 16, 50; Saudi Aramco world, 20;
Nabil Turner, backcover, 18, 38; Mohamed Amin, 32, 42.

First published 2002
Reprinted 2010
© Goodword Books 2010

Goodword Books
1, Nizamuddin West Market, New Delhi-110 013
email: info@goodwordbooks.com
Printed in India

see our complete catalogue at

www.goodwordbooks.com
www.goodword.net

CONTENTS

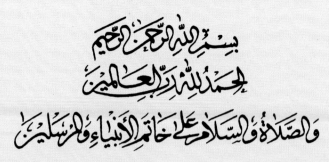

In the name of God, the Most Gracious, the Dispenser of Grace.
All Praise is due to God alone, the Lord of all the Worlds.
Peace and Prayers be upon His Final Prophet and Messenger.

The idea behind this book developed from a series of talks given to Muslim youth during Ramadan, the Muslim month of fasting. I felt that there was a need for a simple informative guide for young Muslims which would also be useful as a teaching resource for parents, teachers and any other interested people, whether they be Muslim or not.

Why Ramadan? Ramadan is a special and blessed month for Muslims. It was the month in which the revelations of the Qur'an descended from God, through Jibra'il (the Angel of Revelation), to the Prophet Muhammad ﷺ. As this month was the starting point of Muhammad ﷺ becoming a Prophet and Messenger, it should also be our starting point to become upholders and followers of the message of Islam. The essence of this month is one's changing to become a better person who remains conscious of God throughout his or her life. Just as the moon changes and is never the same on any day of the fast, we should also change for the better as each day goes by. We should transform ourselves into beacons that clearly illuminate the true teachings of the Qur'an for all to see and help direct humanity out of the depths of darkness onto the path of righteousness.

To be a Muslim is to be a representative of Islam. It is not easy to live up to this responsibility. It requires a lot of sincerity, patience, sacrifice and self-discipline. Ramadan plays a central role in developing and purifying our characters so that we can become sincere servants of God. Ramadan is usually described as a training ground for the remaining eleven months of the year, and those eleven months of the year are a preparation for this blessed month. Therefore, the whole year becomes centred on Ramadan.

This book is just the beginning and I hope, God willing, that through your helpful suggestions, comments and constructive criticisms improvements can be made. I thank God for giving me the ability to complete this work and ask His forgiveness for any mistakes that I have made.

> *"Whoever does not express his gratitude to people*
> *will never be able to be grateful to God."*
> (Hadith – Jami' as-Saghir (vol.2, p.180); Kunuz al-Haqa'iq (p.134))

A special note of thanks to all those who spent their precious time going through the drafts of the Ramadan book: Abdul Aziz, Erica, Khadijah, Marc, Michael, Ridwan, Robina, Salman and Sharon. Their comments and suggestions were invaluable.

Thanks to Harriet for her wonderful illustrations.

Thanks also to Saniyasnain Khan and Goodword Books for taking on this project.

Finally, thanks to my wife for her support and encouragement.

> This book is dedicated to my children, Madinah and Ibrahim,
> who I pray, God willing, will grow up to live Islam in their lives.

October 2000
Glasgow, UK

Javed Ali
javed@andalus.co.uk

هُوَ ٱلَّذِى جَعَلَ ٱلشَّمْسَ ضِيَآءً
وَٱلْقَمَرَ نُورًا وَقَدَّرَهُ مَنَازِلَ لِتَعْلَمُوا عَدَدَ ٱلسِّنِينَ وَٱلْحِسَابَ

*"He it is who has made the Sun [a source of] radiant light
and the moon a light [reflected], and has determined for it
phases so that you may know how to compute the years
and to measure [time]."* [1]

The journey of the sun determines the time during the day, the times of the daily prayers and the daily routine of fasting during Ramadan.

The Phases of the moon allow one to know about the month and its intervals. The Muslim calendar follows the phases of the moon, more commonly known as the lunar calendar. The months of the Ramadan fast and the Hajj (pilgrimage) are based on the lunar calendar.

The lunar months have a bearing on the ebb and flow of the ocean tides. It is also believed to affect human physiology (especially the reproductive cycle) and the way humans behave. The word lunatic comes from the Latin 'Luna' meaning moon.

*"They will ask you about the new moons.
Say: 'they indicate the periods for [various doings of] mankind,
Including the pilgrimage.'"* [2]

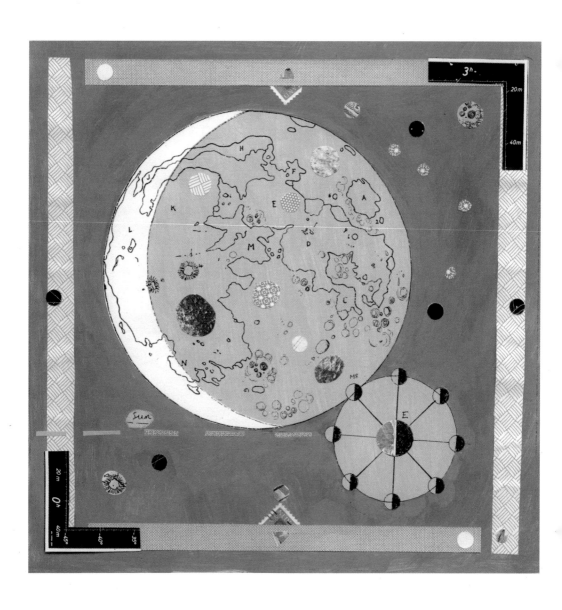

وَٱلْقَمَرَ قَدَّرْنَٰهُ مَنَازِلَ حَتَّىٰ عَادَ كَٱلْعُرْجُونِ ٱلْقَدِيمِ

*"And in the moon,
for which we have determined phases
[which it must traverse]
till it becomes like an old date-stalk
dried up and curved."* [3]

The movement of the moon around the earth gives it different phases. As it moves, its shape changes gradually from a crescent to a full moon, and then it wanes for the remainder of its course until it appears at the end of the month curved and pale like an old date-stalk from a palm tree.

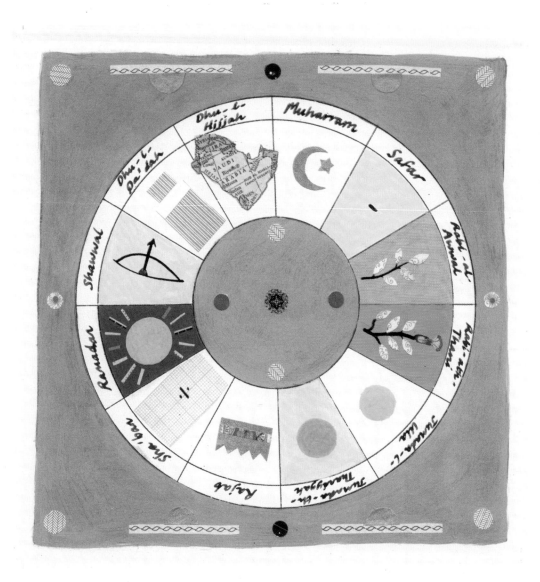

10

THE LUNAR CALENDAR

Each month of the lunar calendar follows a cycle of either twenty-nine or thirty days, beginning when the new crescent moon is sighted at sunset on the western horizon. For a month to be considered as having twenty-nine days the new crescent moon must be sighted after sunset on the twenty-ninth day. If this is not possible due to cloud cover, the month is automatically taken to have thirty days. The Muslim day begins at sunset, when the sun finally disappears below the horizon.

The lunar year being ten or eleven days shorter than the solar year has the effect that over time the Islamic months move back through the seasons, from summer through spring to winter then autumn and back to summer again over a period of approximately thirty four years.

The months of the Islamic year are:

1. Muharram — the sacred month
2. Safar — the month that is void
3. Rabi'al-Awwal — the first spring
4. Rabi'ath-Thani — the second spring
5. Jumadal-Ula — the first month of dryness
6. Jumadath-Thaniyyah — the second month of dryness
7. Rajab — the revered month
8. Sha'ban — the month of division
9. **Ramadan** — the month of intense heat
10. Shawwal — the month of hunting
11. Dhul-Qa'dah — the month of rest
12. Dhul-Hijjah — the month of pilgrimage

شَهْرُ رَمَضَانَ ٱلَّذِىَ أُنزِلَ فِيهِ ٱلْقُرْءَانُ
هُدًى لِّلنَّاسِ وَبَيِّنَتٍ مِّنَ ٱلْهُدَىٰ وَٱلْفُرْقَانِ
فَمَن شَهِدَ مِنكُمُ ٱلشَّهْرَ فَلْيَصُمْهُ

*"It was the month of Ramadan in which the Qur'an was
sent down as guidance for mankind with clear signs
containing guidance, and as the standard by which to
discern the true from the false.
Hence, whoever of you lives to see this month
Shall fast throughout it."* [4]

Ramadan is the ninth month of the Islamic year. It is the month of fasting and the month in which the Qur'an was revealed. It was so named because it originally fell in the height of summer with days of intense heat. Ramadan is derived from the Arabic verb *ramad,* which literally means to bake a sheep in its skin. Similarly, the fasting person living in the hot desert undergoes the sensations of burning in his stomach from the extreme thirst caused by the intense heat of the desert. In the same way, Muslims who fast are slowly burning away their sins.

The month of Ramadan gradually rotates backwards through all seasons and months. The Muslim experiences the discipline of fasting under all kinds of conditions in all seasons. In winter the days are short and cold, making fasting easier. While in summer the long hot days make fasting more difficult. Autumn and spring bring an intermediate situation. All Muslims who fast for a period of about thirty four years, in one place, will have fasted for the same amount of time, no matter where they live.

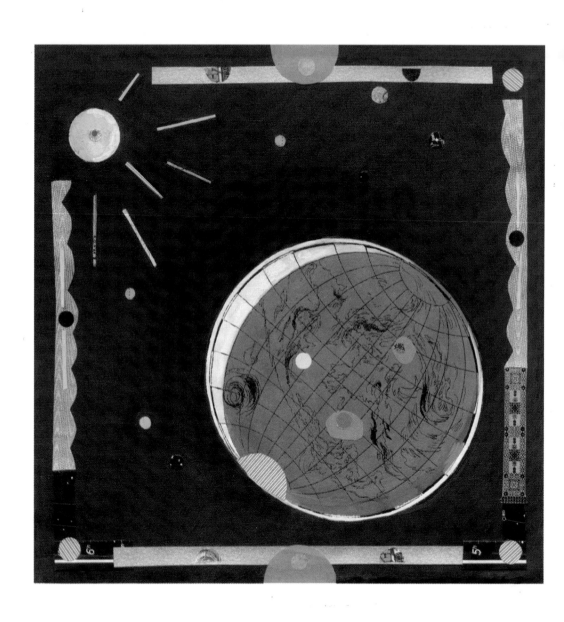

THE START OF RAMADAN

"Fast when you see it
(the new moon of Ramadan)
and break your fast when you see it
(the new moon for Shawwal).
And if the weather is cloudy,
Calculate it (the month of Sha'ban) as thirty days." [5]

The month of Ramadan begins when the crescent of the new moon is sighted, or when the previous month (Sha'ban) reaches thirty days. Fasting begins at dawn the next morning.

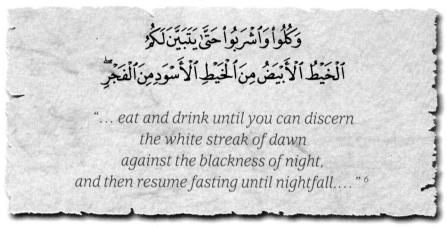

"... eat and drink until you can discern
the white streak of dawn
against the blackness of night,
and then resume fasting until nightfall...." [6]

Dawn is defined as the time when the earliest light is visible on the eastern horizon. This is the time of the morning Adhan (call to prayer). The fast ends at sunset, with the sound of the evening Adhan. Muslims living in non-Muslim countries, particularly those that have cloudier climates, use timetables that include precise times for the start and end of the fast.

SIYAM — FASTING

يَٰٓأَيُّهَا ٱلَّذِينَ ءَامَنُواْ كُتِبَ عَلَيْكُمُ ٱلصِّيَامُ
كَمَا كُتِبَ عَلَى ٱلَّذِينَ مِن قَبْلِكُمْ لَعَلَّكُمْ تَتَّقُونَ

"O you who have attained to faith! Fasting is ordained
for you as it was ordained for those before you,
so that you might remain conscious of God!" [7]

Siyam, one of the pillars of Islam, is an Arabic word which means to abstain. In the month of Ramadan, through the hours of fasting, Muslims abstain from food, drink and sexual activity.

The fast is not only about controlling one's physical appetites but also requires the fasting person to abstain from any form of immoral behaviour. This should be a true characteristic of the behaviour of Muslims at all times.

The Prophet Muhammad ﷺ has said:

> *"Fasting is not abstaining from eating and drinking only, but also from vain speech and foul language. If one of you is being cursed or annoyed, he or she should say, I am fasting. I am fasting."*[8]

> *"God does not need the fast of one who does not abandon false speech, or acting according to his or her false speech."*[9]

> *"Five things spoil a person's fast: lying, slander, backbiting, ungodly oaths and looking with passion."*[10]

Certain acts that are normally permissible, like lawful eating and drinking, become prohibited during the fast and acts that are always forbidden ruin the fast.

Fasting is not something new and is found in other religions. The Muslim fast, however, differs in the number of days, its manner, duration and motive.

The main aim of fasting is to become God-conscious. In addition to this, Muhammad Asad in 'The Message of the Qur'an' mentions how fasting provides an exacting exercise of self-discipline and also how it makes everyone realise, through his own experience, how it feels to be hungry and thirsty, thus gaining a true appreciation of the needs of the poor.[11]

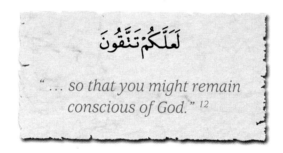

"… *so that you might remain conscious of God.*" [12]

Taqwa taken back to its root word, *waqa*, literally means to preserve, to protect and to keep one safe. The way we protect ourselves is to be always conscious of God, so that we feel that God is with us wherever we are and sees all that we do. God not only sees our actions but also knows what is in our minds. This awareness of God protects us from committing evil, as it is a constant protection from the whisperings and temptations of the Shaytan (Satan).

Taqwa is linked to the heart. The Prophet Muhammad ﷺ used to point to his chest and say:

"Here lies Taqwa." [13]

'Ubayy ibn K'ab understood Taqwa to mean guarding oneself against evil things. Once 'Umar ibn al-Khattab, the second Caliph, asked him to define it and his reply was:

"Have you ever walked along a thorny path?"
"Yes", replied 'Umar.
"What did you do?" 'Ubayy asked.
"I was on my guard", said 'Umar.
"That is Taqwa", said 'Ubayy. [14]

Muhammad Asad defines Taqwa as: " … *the awareness of His all-presence and the desire to mould one's existence in the light of this awareness".* [15]

Taqwa is sometimes translated as the fear of God. Fazlur Rahman says:

> "… Muslims are increasingly discarding the term 'fear of God' because they think the phrase misleading in view of the false picture, widely prevalent in the West until recently – and present even today – of the God of Islam as a capricious dictator or a tyrant, in the light of which 'fear of God' might be indistinguishable from, say, fear of a wolf".[16]

> "Hence Taqwa means to protect oneself against the harmful or evil consequences of one's conduct. If, then, by 'fear of God' one means fear of the consequences of one's actions – whether in this world or the next (fear of punishment of the last day) – one is absolutely right. In other words, it is the fear that comes from an acute sense of responsibility, here and in the hereafter, and not the fear of a wolf or of an uncanny tyrant, for the God of the Qur'an has unbounding mercy – although He also wields dire punishment, both in this world and in the hereafter".[17]

Taqwa makes one alert and cautious of all those things that are harmful; which takes one away from good. A person who has Taqwa is thankful for what he or she has.

وَلِتُكَبِّرُوا اللَّهَ عَلَى مَا هَدَىٰكُمْ
وَلَعَلَّكُمْ تَشْكُرُونَ

"... and that you extol God
for His having guided you aright,
and that you render your thanks [unto Him]." [18]

Shukr (thankfulness) is mentioned in the verses dealing with fasting. To be thankful is a duty of mankind towards God. We thank God for the air we breathe, without which we could not live. We thank God for the water that comes from the skies giving life to all that is dead. Without water we cannot survive. The way that the human body functions is enough to have faith that there is a creator and He deserves to be thanked for giving life to this perfect body. God, out of His mercy, has given people existence and everything that they possess and He can so easily take them away. Is that not enough for which to be thankful? However, very few of His servants are thankful.

Taqwa (God-consciousness) and Shukr cannot be split apart. The one that is conscious of God is thankful for all that he or she has, and knows it is all from God.

INTENTION AND MOTIVE

وَمَآ أُمِرُوٓاْ إِلَّا لِيَعْبُدُواْ ٱللَّهَ مُخْلِصِينَ لَهُ ٱلدِّينَ حُنَفَآءَ

*"And they are ordained nothing else
than to worship God,
sincere in their faith in Him alone ...."* [19]

*"Actions are judged according to the intention behind them,
and for everyone is what he has intended."* [20]

"Whoever does not determine to fast before Fajr will have no fast." [21]

The intention to fast is an essential requirement for the fast to be valid and acceptable. The intention can be made during any part of the night, every night of Ramadan, before Fajr (the obligatory dawn prayer). It does not have to be verbal and can be within one's heart.

*"Every action of the Son of Adam is for him except fasting,
for that is solely for Me. I will give the reward for it."* [22]

Fasting is a form of worship that is hidden from people. No one knows whether a person is fasting or not except God. It is very easy to eat and drink during the fast without anyone knowing. One may be able to fool people, but can one fool God? God knows what is in the hearts and minds of people and it is He who will give the reward for it. One fasts only for God, out of Love and obedience to Him, in order to seek His pleasure.

The Elderly   The Manual Labourer   The Sick

The Child   The Traveller   The Expectant Mother

Every sane, healthy adult who is not travelling should fast the month of Ramadan. There are some situations in which a Muslim is exempt from fasting:

"The pen is raised for three groups [of people] –
that is, they will not be responsible for their actions:
the insane until they become sane,
those who are sleeping until they awaken,
and the young until they reach puberty." [23]

Although children have no obligation to fast until they reach puberty, they are encouraged to participate in fasting up to their capacity according to their age and strength, but in no way should they be forced.

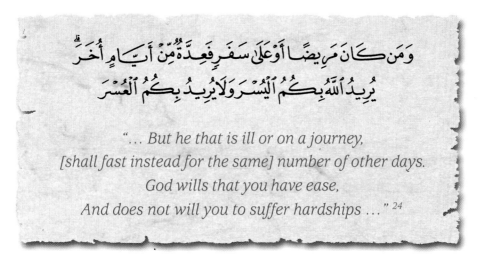

"... But he that is ill or on a journey,
[shall fast instead for the same] number of other days.
God wills that you have ease,
And does not will you to suffer hardships ..." [24]

Muslims who are sick or travelling are afforded an exemption from fasting. God knows the capabilities and limitations of people and does not want any unnecessary hardship or burden to be placed upon them. The days missed, however, should be made up during the year that follows, if this is not possible, then after the next Ramadan.

Women on their monthly periods are exempt from fasting and should also make up the fasts missed.

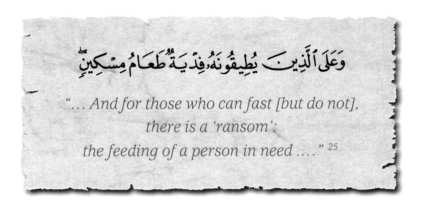

وَعَلَى ٱلَّذِينَ يُطِيقُونَهُۥ فِدۡيَةٞ طَعَامُ مِسۡكِينٖ

"... And for those who can fast [but do not],
there is a 'ransom':
the feeding of a person in need ...." [25]

Initially, in the early days of Islam, Muslims who were able had the choice to fast or not to fast. Those who decided not to fast were to give a ransom in the form of feeding a needy person for every day they did not fast. When the words of the verse, *"Hence, whoever of you lives to see this month shall fast throughout it...."* [26] had been revealed, it then became obligatory for every resident and healthy person to fast the whole month. However, the initial exemption was still kept for the elderly, chronically ill, pregnant and breast-feeding women. If for every day missed a person in need is fed, the days missed do not need to be made up at another time. Also included in this exemption are those who are required to do very heavy or strenuous manual work and have no other means of supporting themselves, as it would cause much hardship for them to fast during any part of the year.

SHAYTAN'S ATTACK

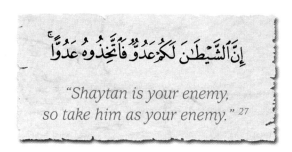

إِنَّ ٱلشَّيْطَنَ لَكُمْ عَدُوٌّ فَٱتَّخِذُوهُ عَدُوًّا

"Shaytan is your enemy,
so take him as your enemy." 27

Shaytan (Satan) started his career at the same time as Adam. Although Shaytan rebelled against God's command, he is in fact a rival and enemy of mankind and not of God. This can be seen in the way Shaytan, full of pride in his disobedience to God's command, fell to a desperate state of utter hopelessness when God sent him out of Paradise.

> *"God said, out you go from the Paradise, for you are cursed, and my curse shall pursue you till the Day of Judgement. He replied, O my Lord! Give me respite till the Day of Resurrection. God replied you have the respite [i.e., you are free to indulge in your activity] till the Day of the Appointed Time [known only to God]. He said, O my Lord! Since You have condemned me, I shall indeed make [all that is evil] seem goodly to them, and shall [try to] lead all of them astray - except Your sincere servants." 28*

Shaytan comes from its Arabic root word, Shatana, which means to distance or be far removed from. Shaytan is the one who distances people from all that is good and true. His aim is to do whatever is in his capability to take people away from the straight path. It is humanity who will either conquer him or be taken over by him and become his followers.

Shaytan has no power or control over humanity but works on our weaknesses. He whispers away at us using every cunning, clever and devious trick known to him.

> *"...Shaytan will say: 'Behold, God promised you something that was bound to come true! I, too, held out [all manner of] promises to you - but I deceived you. Yet I had no power at all over you:*

I but called you - and you responded unto me. Hence, blame not me, but blame yourselves. It is not for me to respond to your cries, nor for you to respond to mine.'" [29]

Shaytan has little or no effect on God's sincere servants whose Taqwa, or God-consciousness, protects them and keeps them alert and aware of his attack.

The Prophet Muhammad ﷺ said:

"Fasting is like a shield...." [30]

A shield is a form of protection. It protects one from his or her enemy's attack. Fasting is a protection from committing evil by shielding the senses and limbs from wrongdoing. The tongue does not say anything that displeases God. The eye does not see anything that displeases God. The ear does not hear anything that displeases God. The hands refrain themselves from doing anything that displeases God. The feet do not go towards any place that displeases God.

"The blessed month has come to you.
God has made fasting obligatory upon you.
During it, the gates to Paradise are opened
and the gates to Hellfire are locked,
and the Shaytans are chained." [31]

The month of Ramadan is a special month, as it is the only month of the year where the Shaytan and his followers are not allowed to roam freely. It is up to us to decide whether we will do good or evil actions, as in reality is the case during the whole year. If one is influenced by the constant whisperings and temptations of the Shaytan and follows his footsteps during the other eleven months, then surely one will also continue this way throughout Ramadan.

Fasting develops Taqwa, discipline and self-control. Man is at a constant struggle with the self and fasting is a means of protecting and elevating the self from all forms of actions and thoughts that take one away from what is good and true.

FORGETFULNESS

"If somebody eats or drinks forgetfully,
then he should complete his fast,
for what he has eaten or drunk
has been given to him by God." [32]

At the beginning of Ramadan, especially during the first few days before a routine of fasting can be established, it is very easy for Muslims to forget that they are fasting and eat and drink by accident. Such forgetfulness does not break the fast, which is recommenced immediately after one realises what has happened.

وَإِذَا سَأَلَكَ عِبَادِى عَنِّى فَإِنِّى قَرِيبٌ
أُجِيبُ دَعْوَةَ الدَّاعِ إِذَا دَعَانِ فَلْيَسْتَجِيبُواْ لِى
وَلْيُؤْمِنُواْ بِى لَعَلَّهُمْ يَرْشُدُونَ

"And if My Servants ask you about Me - behold,
I am near; I respond to the call of him who calls,
whenever he calls unto Me:
let them, then, respond unto Me, and believe in Me,
so that they might follow the right way." [33]

God is very near to humanity and will always remain near. He is closer to us than we are to our own jugular vein: the vein that carries blood from the head to the heart. It is not God who is far; it is we who are far from God. We only have to ask sincerely and God will answer.

The human being, *Insan*, comes from the Arabic root word *nasiya* meaning 'to forget'. We are constantly forgetting the favours God has given us and easily stray away from the straight path. To be near to God is to constantly remember and supplicate Him. In doing so one remains firm in one's faith towards God and follows the true way.

"The pre-dawn meal is blessed,
so do not neglect it even if you only take a sip of water.
Verily, God and the Angels bless those who have pre-dawn meals." [34]

Just before the commencement of the fast, at the first light of dawn, Muslims take a morning meal called Suhur. This strengthens the fasting person and helps him endure and cope with the hardships of the fast. It is also a time for Muslims to thank God for having food and drink; soon they will feel how it is to live without either during the fast.

"The people will always be with the good
as long as they hasten the breaking of the fast
and delay the taking of the morning meal." [35]

It was the practice of the Prophet Muhammad ﷺ to delay Suhur, to eat and drink as close as possible to the time of the start of the fast and to break the fast quickly at the end of the time of the fast.

IFTAR —
BREAKING THE FAST

"The people will always be with the good
as long as they hasten in breaking the fast." [36]

Shortly before the Iftar, breaking of the fast, is a time for all Muslims to consciously reflect and think about the day that they have fasted. As each day of the fast goes by, one continuously strives to improve on the previous day with the hope that God will accept one's fast. On this point, Imam al-Ghazali has said:

"... that their heart should remain in a state of suspense between
fear and hope, after the daily ending of the prescribed fast,
because they do not know whether or not their prescribed fast
will be accepted. Will they be among the friends of God or
among the rejected by God? They should remain in such a state
of suspense after every act of worship."[37]

The best way for Muslims to make use of this valuable time is for them to sincerely supplicate to their Lord asking Him to accept their fast. Supplications, before the fast is broken, are surely answered:

"Three people will not have their supplications rejected:
a fasting person until he breaks his fast,
a just ruler and an oppressed person." [38]

The words of the supplication of the Prophet Muhammad ﷺ, when breaking his fasts, give an indication of the kind of discomfort he underwent when fasting in the Arabian summer with its scorching heat:

"Gone is the thirst,
moist are the veins,
and assured is the reward,
if it be the will of God."[39]

At other times the Prophet Muhammad ﷺ would simply say:

"O God, for you I have fasted,
and with what you have provided,
do I break my fast."[40]

The Prophet Muhammad ﷺ used to eat and drink very little before the prayer; it is preferable to eat before drinking. He used to break his fast with an odd number of dates and if that was not available with some water.

"If one of you is fasting,
he should break his fast with dates.
If dates are not available,
then with water, for water is purifying." [41]

After the Maghrib prayer (the obligatory prayer immediately after sunset) the main meal is usually served. There is a great reward and blessing for those who invite and share their food with others. The Prophet Muhammad ﷺ has said:

"'Whosoever feeds a person performing the prescribed fast in order to end the fast at sunset, for him there shall be forgiveness of his sins and emancipation from the hell-fire, and for him shall be the same reward as for him whom he fed, without that person's reward being diminished in the least.'

Thereupon we said, 'Oh Messenger of God, not all of us possess
the means whereby we can provide enough for a prescribed
fasting person to break the prescribed fast.' The Messenger
replied, 'God grants this same reward to one who gives a person
who is performing the prescribed fast a single date or a drink
of water or a sip of milk to end the prescribed fast.'"[42]

Unfortunately, many Muslims seem to gain more weight during Ramadan than in any other month. The extravagant overeating of different varieties of food, rarely prepared during the rest of the year, goes against the whole principle of fasting. The Iftar, to some, has just become a party celebrating the completing of the fast. What use is fasting during the day, when one is going to fill his belly full with food and drink at Iftar and literally sleep during the night prayers. If it is not recommended for us to fill our belly full during any other part of the year, then why should one do so in Ramadan? Imam al-Ghazali writes very strongly about the overeating of lawful food at Iftar. He says:

> "For there is no vessel more abominable unto God than a belly stuffed with lawful food."[43]

> "It has thus become the custom to store up all the food for the month of Ramadan, wherein more food and drink are devoured than in several months. Yet it is well known that the purpose of prescribed fasting is hunger and suppression of lust so that the self might be able to attain piety. If the stomach were not given any food from the early morning until the evening so that its appetite became aroused and its desire increased and then it were fed with delicacies and stuffed to satiety therewith, its pleasure would be enhanced and vitality doubled, consequently giving rise to passions otherwise dormant. The spirit as well as the secret of prescribed fasting is to weaken the flesh, which is the human ego's tool for turning the self back to wrongdoing. The weakening of the flesh is never achieved unless a person reduces his food to the amount of food which he would have eaten in the evening if he were not fasting." [44]

TARAWIH —
SPECIAL NIGHT PRAYERS

"Whoever prayed at night, the whole month of Ramadan,
out of sincere faith and hoping for a reward from God,
then all of his previous wrong actions will be forgiven." [45]

The special night prayers during Ramadan are called Tarawih. They are performed after the obligatory Isha prayer and can be offered until the end of the night preferably before the Witr prayer, the last prayer of the night. Tarawih prayers are usually performed in sets of two rakahs (a rakah being one cycle of the prayer). Tarawih means 'to rest'; after every four rakahs of prayer there is a brief rest.

The usual cultural practice among Muslims, every night of the fast, is for the Imam (one who leads the prayer) who is usually a Hafiz (one who has memorised the Qur'an from start to finish) to recite one thirtieth of the Qur'an spread over eight or twenty rakahs (those praying eight rakahs have longer recitations in each rakah); so that by the end of Ramadan the whole Qur'an would have been recited. These prayers are not obligatory but Muslims are encouraged to offer them because of the great reward associated with this blessed month.

The Tarawih prayer is a means of spiritually drawing closer to God. Standing sincerely listening to the recitation of the Qur'an should awaken the heart of the listener. Every night that we stand in prayer, we become much stronger in our consciousness of God. This causes our behaviour to change, reflecting moral and spiritual growth, which can be seen through our actions during each day of the fast and continuing throughout the year.

We should reflect upon our actions at all times and make sure that the Tarawih prayer has a profound effect on our hearts, changing the way we think, understand and behave. As one pious scholar said:

"Reflection is the lamp of the heart;
if it departs the heart will have no light." [46]

I'TIKAF —
RETREAT TO A MOSQUE

"The Prophet Muhammad ﷺ used to practise I'tikaf
in the last ten days of Ramadan".[47]

I'tikaf literally means to stay in a place. It was the practice of the Prophet Muhammad ﷺ to spend a certain number of days, especially the last ten days of Ramadan, in the environs of the mosque devoting himself exclusively to prayer and remembrance of God.

Secluding oneself in the mosque, away from all worldly affairs, while concentrating solely on prayer and devotion develops a deep consciousness of God. The heart becomes attached to God.

Ibn Qayyim al-Jawziyya says: *"A state is reached in which all fears, hopes and apprehensions are superseded by the love and remembrance of God. Every anxiety is transformed into the anxiety for Him. Every thought and feeling is blended with the eagerness to gain His nearness and earn His good favour. Devotion to the Almighty is generated instead of devotion to this world. It becomes the provision for the grave where there will be neither a friend nor a helper. This is the high aim and purpose of I'tikaf which is the speciality of the most sublime part of Ramadan: the last ten days".*[48]

Through I'tikaf one attains peace of mind and the purification of the heart. This will be achieved not only through constant prayer and devotion but also by speaking well of others and avoiding foolish talks, refraining from arguing and getting angry or speaking badly about anyone. God has placed the tongue in the mouth as a prisoner; the rows of teeth are the bars that clamp shut, the jaws the cell walls and the lips that seal the mouth are the final confinement from freedom. One should only allow the tongue freedom by letting it out in good behaviour. Imam Ali, a companion of the Prophet Muhammad ﷺ and a Caliph in Islam, said: *"The tongue is like a lion - if you let it run free it will wound someone".*[49] Beware; the tongue can so easily lead one to hell. This restraint of the tongue does not only apply to those in I'tikaf but to all Muslims that fast and should be a characteristic of their behaviour at all times.

"God does not need the fast of one who does not abandon false speech,
or acting according to his false speech." [50]

I'tikaf is the only sure means of seeking and finding Lailat-ul-Qadr, a night which is greater in worth than a thousand months.

LAILAT-UL-QADR —
THE NIGHT OF POWER

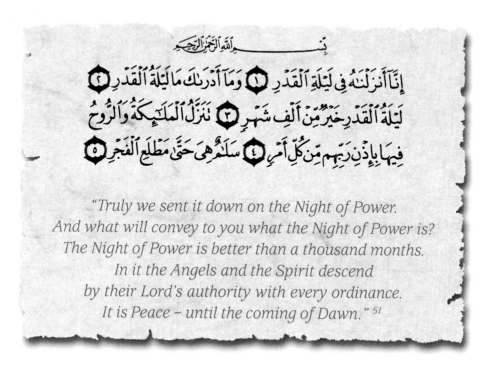

> "Truly we sent it down on the Night of Power.
> And what will convey to you what the Night of Power is?
> The Night of Power is better than a thousand months.
> In it the Angels and the Spirit descend
> by their Lord's authority with every ordinance.
> It is Peace – until the coming of Dawn." [51]

Lailat-ul-Qadr is one day in a year, every year, in the last ten days of the month of Ramadan. No one is definitely sure exactly what day it is from the known last ten days. Some say it is the twenty-seventh of the month and others say it varies from year to year, but always among the last ten days.

The Prophet Muhammad ﷺ has said:

> "Seek the Night of Power in the last ten days of Ramadan." [52]

> "Seek the Night of Power in an odd [night]
> among the last ten [nights] of Ramadan." [53]

The Prophet Muhammad ﷺ came out to inform us about the Night of Power, but two Muslims were quarrelling with each other. So, the Prophet Muhammad ﷺ said, *"I came out to inform you about the Night of Power but such and such persons were quarrelling, so the news about it had been taken away; yet that might be for your own good, so search for it on the ninth, seventh and the fifth."* [54]

Abu Sa'id al-khudri was then asked, "what is the ninth, seventh and fifth?" He explained this by saying:

"When twenty one (nights) are over and the twenty second begins, it is the ninth, and when twenty three (nights) are over, that which follows (the last night) is the seventh, and when twenty five nights are over, what follows it is the fifth." [55]

The counting of the odd nights in the last ten days starts from the end of the month. The day starts at sunset, the end of the previous days fast, and the fast begins at dawn. If the month is twenty nine days, the new crescent moon being sighted, then the ninth, seventh and fifth would differ from a month of thirty days.

Such a great night, a night better and more worthy than a thousand months deserves to be found and the only way to be certain of finding it is to spend all ten nights in the sincere worship of one's Lord.

Lail means night and Qadr taken back to its root, Qadara, means to be able, have power over, measure or determine the size or quantity of something.

"The word Qadar comes from the same root as Qadir, which is a divine name that we have been translating as 'Powerful'. The noun Qudra, which designates the divine attribute of power, is close to Qadar both in derivation and meaning. To have power is to have the ability or capacity to do or make something, to perform an act, to achieve a goal. God, the Qur'an tells us repeatedly, 'is powerful over all things', so his power – in contrast to ours – is unlimited.

Qadar is sometimes used synonymously with Qudra, so it also means 'power' and 'ability'. But the word Qadar puts stress on the basic meaning of the root, which is to measure or determine the size or quantity of something. This may be done physically, with a scale or a tape measure, or it may be done mentally, through computation and reckoning. The term may mean not only 'to take something's measure', but also 'to determine its measure'. To measure something, in this sense, is to control it and govern it, to have power over it. Hence we come back to power." [56]

Lailat-ul-Qadr is usually translated as the Night of Power or the Night of Destiny and is also described as the Night of Grandeur or Majesty or an Honourable Night. All these signify the measure of greatness of such a night due to the revelation of the Qur'an.

It is the night in which the revelation of the Qur'an started, bringing light to those that were blind to the truth. It was during this night that the career of Muhammad the man, as Muhammad the Prophet of God began, who was charged with conveying the message not just to his own people but also to the whole of humanity. It would be a message that would take people out of the depths of darkness onto the path illuminating the truth. Also during this night the angels descend to the God-loving people who are sincerely striving in worship, hoping to receive the Mercy of God. In just a few words, the Prophet Muhammad ﷺ has shown us the best way to supplicate to our Lord in this great Night:

"O God, you are Pardoning and love to Pardon,
so Pardon me." [57]

The Arabic word *'afw*, translated here as Pardon, means to obliterate, destroy, eliminate one's wrong actions.

The Mercy of God is so great and so much during this night that peace and security reign until the rise of dawn. But if the light of this night reaches our hearts, then it will always remain there.

The Prophet Muhammad ﷺ has said:

"One who spends the Night of Power in worship,
with faith and hoping for its reward,
will have all of one's previous wrong actions forgiven." [58]

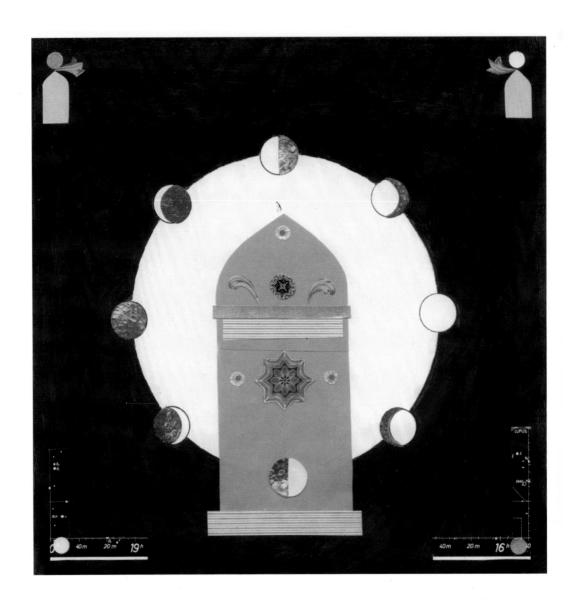

ZAKAT-UL-FITR

"The Messenger of God ✿ enjoined Zakat-ul-fitr
on the one who fasts to shield one's self
from any indecent act or speech,
and for the purpose of providing food for the needy." [59]

Zakah, the mandatory giving of alms, taken back to its root, *Zaka*, means to increase, purify and bless. The one who gives Zakah increases or grows in purification and is blessed by God. Zakah is the right of God to a Muslim's wealth. Once the Zakah is given, the remaining wealth of the person becomes pure and legitimate.

> *"The basic idea behind Zakat is that people purify their wealth*
> *by giving a share of it to God. Just as ablutions purify the body*
> *and Salat purifies the soul, so Zakat purifies possessions and*
> *makes them pleasing to God."* [60]

Zakat-ul-Fitr is specifically related to the month of fasting and is given before the special prayer for 'Id. Zakat-ul-Fitr perfects the fast of Ramadan and purifies the fast from any indecent act or speech.

It is obligatory on all Muslims: young, old, male and female. Every adult Muslim who possesses over and above what is needed as basic food for the duration of one day and night must pay Zakat-ul-Fitr, approximately 3 kg of dates or barley or its equivalent value in money. It is usually the head of the household who collects the Zakatul-fitr for himself and his dependents and then passes it on to the Muslim community to distribute it.

It is used to help the poor and needy. The earlier it is given the easier it is to make arrangements to help them, so that they can also partake in the celebrations of 'Id without any difficulties.

'ID-UL-FITR

"O Muslims, this is our festival." [61]

'Id-ul-Fitr means the festival of the breaking of the fast. It follows the day when the new moon is sighted signifying the end of the month of Ramadan and the start of the month of Shawwal. The festival starts on the first day of Shawwal and lasts for three days.

The festival is marked by a special 'Id prayer performed by the whole community. Muslims thank God for His blessings during the month of Ramadan and ask God to accept their fasts. After the 'Id prayer, Muslims greet each other with the following saying: *"May God accept it (the fast of Ramadan) from me and you."* [62]

The 'Id is a time for Muslims to come together forgiving one another for their weaknesses and strengthening the bonds of brotherhood. True unity should be initiated on the 'Id and continue until the next, which should be stronger than the previous year. Muslims should be people who unite, not divide, and be tolerant to those who hold differing views.

The 'Id is a happy time and the festivities should outstretch the Muslim community into the wider non-Muslim society. Muslims from different countries with varying cultures celebrate the 'Id in a variety of ways. This diversity in unity is a wonderful thing and emphasises the coming of Islam for all of humanity and not just for a particular people.

Those Muslims who truly benefit from the fasting month are the ones who become conscious of God throughout their lives. They are the ones who surrender themselves to God out of love and devotion. They are the ones who show mercy and tolerance to one another and attain true happiness and peace within their hearts. Surely they are the ones who will truly enjoy and share their happiness with others during the 'Id.

EXTRA VOLUNTARY FASTS

A man came to the Prophet Muhammad ﷺ and said:

"O Messenger of God,
tell me what God requires of me as regards fasting."
He answered, "the Month of Ramadan."
The man asked: "Is there any other [fast]?
The Prophet Muhammad ﷺ answered:
"No, unless you do so voluntarily." [63]

Apart from the prescribed fast of Ramadan, Muslims can fast voluntarily. The Prophet Muhammad ﷺ fasted often and encouraged others to do extra voluntary fasts at other times of the year.

THE SIX FASTS OF SHAWWAL

"Whoever fasts during the month of Ramadan
and then follows it with six days of Shawwal
will be [rewarded] as if he had fasted the entire year." [64]

Immediately after Ramadan, it was the practice of the Prophet Muhammad ﷺ to fast six days during the month of Shawwal. These fasts can be kept consecutively, one day after another, or during any six days of the month apart from the day of 'Id, the first day of the month.

AFTER RAMADAN: WHAT NEXT?
ˎ REFLECT AND CHANGE ˎ

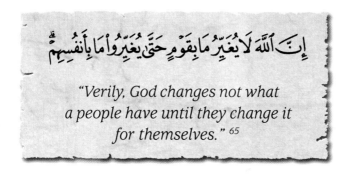

إِنَّ ٱللَّهَ لَا يُغَيِّرُ مَا بِقَوْمٍ حَتَّىٰ يُغَيِّرُوا۟ مَا بِأَنفُسِهِمْ

*"Verily, God changes not what
a people have until they change it
for themselves."* [65]

This book ends as it started. Ramadan is all about change and it brings about a psychological, spiritual and physical change in our lives. The decision to change is ours. As Ramadan leaves us behind we can either change for the better or return to the state we were in before. Those who strive to change will continue to change even though Ramadan is over.

> *"Don't be like a wave that only makes a noise when it hits the beach. Be like a flood that changes the world every time it comes."* [66]

Everyday that we live should be a careful look at the day we leave behind. Reflecting on each day's events helps us to recognise our weaknesses and strengths, make our lives more meaningful and focused, and most importantly, to see whether or not we are creating an awareness of God in our lives.

> *"Reflection is the lamp of the heart;
> If it departs the heart will have no light."* [67]

"O You who have attained to faith! Be ever steadfast in your devotion to God, bearing witness to the truth in all equity: and never let hatred of anyone lead you into the sin of deviating from justice. Be Just: this is closest to being God-conscious. And remain conscious of God: verily, God is aware of all that you do." [68]

GLOSSARY

"Islam has been built upon five [pillars]:
testifying that there is no god but Allah and that Muhammad is
the Messenger of Allah, performing the Salah, paying the Zakah,
making the Hajj to the House, and fasting in Ramadan."

Hadith – Related by Al-Bukhari and Muslim.

Adhan	The call to Salah (formal prayer in Islam).
Allah	The Arabic name for God.
Akhirah	Literally means that which is Last, referring to the Next World, the Final Abode, the Hereafter.
Ayah	Ayah in Arabic means sign. A sign directs and leads people towards something. A verse in the Qur'an is also called an Ayah as it shows and leads people towards God.
Dunya	The present world as opposed to the Next World or the Akhirah.
Fajr	The Salah performed between first light and sunrise.
Hadith	A report of word or actions attributable to the Prophet.
Hafiz	The one who protects and preserves the whole Qur'an through Memorisation.
Hajj	The annual pilgrimage to Makkah, compulsory for those who have the means to perform it. One of the five pillars of Islam.
'Id	Festival.
'Id-ul-Fitr	The festival to mark the end of Ramadan, the month of fasting.
Iftar	The breaking of the fast.
Imam	The one who leads the Salah, formal prayer in Islam.
Insan	Human being.
Islam	Surrendering oneself to God.
I'tikaf	Literally means to stay in a place. It refers to staying in the Mosque during the last ten days of Ramadan for contemplation, worship and attempting to get nearer to God.

Jibra'il	The Angel Gabriel, the Angel of Revelation, who brought the revelations of the Qur'an to the Prophet Muhammad.
Lailat-ul-Qadr	The Night of Power or Destiny.
Masjid	Place of Prostration, Mosque.
Muslim	One who surrenders himself to God.
Qur'an	The divine message revealed to the Prophet Muhammad.
Rakah	A sequence of actions or movements repeated cyclically in the performance of the Salah.
Ramadan	The ninth month of the Islamic year. The month of Fasting.
Suhur	Light traditional meal taken before commencing a day's fasting in Ramadan.
Salah	Formal prayer in Islam, particularly the five obligatory prayers which constitute one of the pillars of Islam.
Sha'ban	The month before Ramadan.
Shawwal	The month after Ramadan.
Shaytan	The Devil, Satan.
Shukr	Thankfulness.
Siyam	Literally means to abstain. It refers to Ramadan where Muslims, during the hours of fasting, abstain from food, drink and sexual activity.
Surah	Literally means a fence, enclosure or any part of a structure. A chapter of the Qur'an.
Tarawih	A sequence of Rakahs performed after Isha prayer in Ramadan, usually with 1/30th part of the Qur'an recited every night, thus the entire Qur'an is recited during the month.
Taqwa	God-consciousness, which inspires a person to be on guard against wrong action and eager for actions that please God.
Witr	Uneven, odd number. The last prayer of the night.
Zakah	That part of a Muslim's wealth paid in charity as a compulsory annual tax to purify the remainder. One of the five pillars of Islam.

NOTES

1 The Qur'an – Surah 10, Yunus (Jonah), Ayah 5.
2 The Qur'an – Surah 2, Al-Baqarah (The Cow), Ayah 189.
3 The Qur'an – Surah 36, Ya Sin, Ayah 39.
4 The Qur'an – Surah 2, Al-Baqarah (The Cow), Ayah 185.
5 Hadith – Related by Al-Bukhari and Muslim.
6 The Qur'an – Surah 2, Al-Baqarah (The Cow), Ayah 187.
7 The Qur'an – Surah 2, Al-Baqarah (The Cow), Ayah 183.
8 Hadith – Related by Ibn Khuzaimah, Ibn Hibban and Al-Hakim.
9 Hadith – Related by Al-Bukhari and others except Muslim.
10 Hadith – Mentioned in the book, 'As-Siyam – Fasting' by Al-Bahay al-Kholy, page 31.
11 Muhammad Asad, The Message of the Qur'an, see footnote 155, page 38-39.
12 The Qur'an – Surah 2, Al-Baqarah (The Cow), Ayah 183.
13 Hadith – Related by Muslim, At-Tirmidhi and Ahmad.
14 Extract taken from the book, 'As-Siyam – Fasting' by Al-Bahay al-Kholy, page 13.
15 Muhammad Asad, The Message of the Qur'an, see footnote 2, page 3.
16 Fazlur Rahman, Major Themes of the Qur'an, chapter 2, page 28.
17 Ibid, chapter 2, page 29.
18 The Qur'an – Surah 2, Al-Baqarah (The Cow), Ayah 185.
19 The Qur'an – Surah 98, Al-Bayyinah (The Clear Sign), Ayah 5.
20 Hadith – Related by Al-Bukhari and Muslim.
21 Hadith – Related by Ahmad, an-Nasa'I, At-Tirmidhi, Abu Dawud and Ibn Majah.
22 Hadith – Related by Muslim.
23 Hadith – Related by Ahmad, Abu Dawud and At-Tirmidhi.
24 The Qur'an – Surah 2, Al-Baqarah (The Cow), Ayah 185.
25 The Qur'an – Surah 2, Al-Baqarah (The Cow), Ayah 184.
26 The Qur'an – Surah 2, Al-Baqarah (The Cow), Ayah 185.
27 The Qur'an – Surah 35, Al-Fatir (The Originator), Ayah 6.
28 The Qur'an – Surah 15, Al-Hijr, Ayah 34-40.
29 The Qur'an – Surah 14, Ibrahim (Abraham), Ayah 22.
30 Hadith – Related by Muslim.
31 Hadith – Related by Ahmad, An-Nasa'i and Al-Baihaqi.
32 Hadith – Related by Al-Bukhari and others.
33 The Qur'an – Surah 2, Al-Baqarah (The Cow), Ayah 186.
34 Hadith – Related by Ahmad.
35 Hadith – Related by Al-Bukhari and Muslim.
36 Hadith – Related by Al-Bukhari and Muslim.
37 Imam al-Ghazali, 'On the Mysteries of Prescribed Fasting', extract taken from the book, 'Ramadan Motivating Believers into Action', edited by Laleh Bakhtar, chapter 2, page 25.
38 Hadith – Related by At-Tirmidhi.
39 Hadith – Related by Abu Dawud.
40 Hadith – Related by Abu Dawud.
41 Hadith – Related by Ahmad and At-Tirmidhi.
42 Hadith – Related by Al-Bukhari.
43 Imam al-Ghazali, 'On the Mysteries of Prescribed Fasting', extract taken from the book, 'Ramadan Motivating Believers into Action', edited by Laleh Bakhtar, chapter 2, page 24.
44 Ibid.
45 Hadith – Related by Al-Bukhari and others.
46 Imam al-Haddad, 'The Book of Assistance', chapter 9, page 31.
47 Hadith – Related by Al-Bukhari, Abu Dawud and Ibn Majah.
48 Ibn Qayyim, Zad al-Ma'ad, pages 176 & 178, extract taken from the book, 'Ramadan Motivating Believers to Action', edited by Laleh Bakhtar, chapter 23, page 257.
49 Shaykh Fadhlalla Haeri, 'The Sayings & Wisdom of Imam Ali', chapter 6, page 66.
50 Hadith – Related by Al-Bukhari and others except Muslim.
51 The Qur'an – Surah 97, Al-Qadr (Power), Ayah1-5.
52 Hadith – Related by Muslim.
53 Hadith – Related by Al-Bukhari.
54 Hadith – Related by Al-Bukhari and Muslim.
55 Hadith – Related by Muslim.
56 William Chittick and Sachiko Murata, 'The Vision of Islam', chapter 3, page 104.
57 Hadith – Related by Ahmad, Ibn Majah and At-Tirmidhi.
58 Hadith – Related by Al-Bukhari and Muslim.
59 Hadith – Related by Abu Dawud, Ibn Majah and ad-Daraqutni.
60 William Chittick and Sachiko Murata, 'The Vision of Islam', chapter 1, page 16.
61 Hadith – Related by Muslim.
62 Hadith – mentioned in 'Fiqh us-Sunnah' by Sayyid Sabiq, Vol. 2, page 154 (Eng. trans.).
63 Ibid. Vol. 3, page 109.
64 Hadith – Related by Muslim and others except for Al-Bukhari and An-Nasa'i.
65 The Qur'an – Surah 13, Ar-Ra'd (Thunder), Ayah 12.
66 Muhammad Iqbal, source not known.
67 Imam al-Haddad, 'The Book of Assistance', chapter 9, page 31.
68 The Qur'an – Surah 5, Al-Ma'idah (The Repast), Ayah 8.